PRA`

CONQUEST 1

Deliverance Prayers Manual for Conquerors in Christ

Adedamola Adedokun Olofa

ATTRIBUTION

He shall call upon me, and I will answer him: I will be with him in trouble; I will deliver him, and honour him.— Psa_91:15

DEDICATION

*In every generation, God raises a Gospel-General for His people.
In this generation, Dr. D.K. Olukoya is raised by the Lord of Host,
as one of the greatest end time Generals for the revival of the
apostolic signs, Holy Ghost fireworks and unlimited
demonstration of the power of God to save, to heal and to
deliver to the uttermost.
He keeps imparting on us what the Lord has imparted on you.
You shall never fall in Jesus name. Amen.*

Thank you, Daddy DKO.

Cover designed by **KDP Cover Designer**

Printed in the United States of America

CONTENTS

PRAYER OF MERCY

Have mercy upon me, O God, according to thy loving kindness:

Psalms 51:1a

Mercy *pacifies* God. And, mercy also *preserves*, *protects*, *provides* and *promotes* you.

The Canaanitish woman cried, *"...Have mercy on me, O Lord, thou Son of David; my daughter is grievously vexed with a devil."* And her daughter got deliverance.

The Blind Bartimaeus cried out, *"... Jesus, thou Son of David, have mercy on me."* And he got her sight restored.

Epraphroditus *was sick nigh unto death* but received divine mercy. And he got healed.

So, you see, aside from the 5Ps of mercy, mercy brings deliverance, healing, restores vision, saves from death, etc.

Or maybe, your mind is nudging you that you need to reconcile with God? Or it seems as if heavens are shut or the whole world appears to be falling on you alone? And you have prayed all manners of prayers without answers? Does it not look as if God is not there anymore?

Pray for His mercy now. And you will get *yours* too.

TEXT:

2Chronicles 7:14; Philippians 2:27; Mark 10:47- 48, Matthew 15:22; Micah 7:19; Lam 3:22, Daniel 9:9

CONFESSION:

To the chief Musician, A Psalm of David, when Nathan the prophet came unto him, after he had gone in to Bathsheba. Have mercy upon me, O God, according to thy loving kindness: according unto the multitude of thy tender mercies blot out my transgressions. Psalms 51:1

SING PRAISES

PRAYER POINTS

[*On your knees, repeat each of points 1 - 6 severally*]

1. Blood of Jesus Christ, plead mercy upon my destiny.

2. By the power in the blood of Jesus Christ, I come to the throne of mercy.

3. Mercy of God, appear unto me in this prayer in the name of Jesus Christ.

4. God of love, God of mercy, You are my Father, pardon all my sins, overlook my iniquities, shortcomings, trespasses and transgressions in the name of Jesus Christ.

5. Fountain of the blood of Jesus Christ, wash away the stains and the stench of my sins.

6. Repercussions of sins in my life, building a gulf between me and my Maker; be removed by the mercy of God.

7. Blood of Jesus Christ, redeem my glory from satanic transactions.

8. Oh Lord my Father, redeem me from negative self-transactions in the name of Jesus Christ.

9. If I had sold myself out to the enemies, mercy of God, ransom me in the name of Jesus Christ.

10. Oh Lord my Father, if I am my own enemy; have mercy and redirect me in the name of Jesus Christ.

11. I have been on one spot for too long, Mercy of God, appear and move me forward in the name of Jesus Christ.

12. Mercy of God, shut the doors of defeat I have opened to the enemies of my glory in the name of Jesus Christ.

13. Mercy of God, terminate self-destructive habits in my life in the name of Jesus Christ.

14. Mercy of the Lord, appear unto me, redirect the routes of my life unto fulfilment in the name of Jesus Christ.

15. Parental grievances holding down the eagle of my destiny from flying, the mercy of God has pleaded for me, loose your hold in the name of Jesus Christ.

16. Sexual pollution in the very acts, the blood of Jesus Christ is speaking mercy for me, be flushed out by the blood of Jesus Christ.

17. Mercy spoken by the voice of the blood of Jesus Christ, terminate divine curses in my life in the name of Jesus Christ.

18. Mercy of God, turn curses in my life to blessings in the name of Jesus Christ.

19. Mercy from above, move me from zero to zenith in the name of Jesus Christ.

20. Mercy of God, turn failures in my life to good success in the name of Jesus Christ.

21. Shaven-off hair of my Samson; grow again by the mercy of the Lord in the name of Jesus Christ.

22. Gorged-out eyeballs of my Samson, by the mercy of the Lord, receive divine replacement in the name of Jesus Christ.

23. I receive mercy over the bondage of corruption in the name of Jesus Christ.

24. In your mercy, O Lord, hide me in the hollow of your hands, in the name of Jesus Christ.

25. Mercy of the Lord, dissolve curses of the aggrieved raging in my life in the name Jesus Christ.

26. Voice of the blood of Jesus Christ, speak mercy on my behalf in the name of Jesus Christ.

27. Mercy of the Lord, establish my calling, destiny, ministry and family in righteousness, favour, holiness, goodness, power, glory, fire, anointing and back it up with miracles, sign and wonders in the name of Jesus Christ.

28. My father, baptize me with uncommon mercy, in the name of Jesus Christ.

29. Magnet of mercy, attract favour into my life in the name of Jesus.

30. I recover my wasted years by the mercy of the Lord Jesus Christ.

SING WORSHIP TO THE LORD FOR 5 MINUTES FOR HIS MERCY

PRAYING GENESIS 1 - A NEW BEGINNING!

(He) will even make a way in the wilderness, and rivers in the

desert. Isaiah 43:19b

This prayer, Praying Genesis 1 is ideal for committing a New Year, new ventures, new appointments, new marriage, etc.

It is also an ideal prayer for starting all over (maybe after a fall)

Please note, praying with Bible references is one of the most authoritative approaches to prayers and surest way of making the adversary to bow out faster. Mathew 4:4-11

Praying the Bible references is known to be prophetic.

TEXT:

Genesis 1:1 – 3; Psalms 11:3, Isaiah 54:11-12

CONFESSION:

Behold, (The Lord) will do a new thing; now it shall spring forth; shall (I) not know it? (He) will even make a way in the wilderness, and rivers in the desert. Isaiah 43:19

SING PRAISES

PRAYER POINTS

GENESIS 1:

¹ *In the beginning God created the heaven and the earth.*

1. My foundations; drink the blood of Jesus Christ.

2. Blood of Jesus Christ, speak mercy to my foundations.

3. My foundations, receive fire in the name of Jesus Christ.

² *And the earth was without form, and void; and darkness was upon the face of the deep. And the Spirit of God moved upon the face of the waters.*

4. Witchcraft manipulations at the beginning of my destiny, be reversed by fire in the name of Jesus Christ.

5. Anything stolen at the beginning of my life; be restored by fire in the name of Jesus Christ.

6. Light of God; disgrace the darkness in my foundations, in the name of Jesus Christ.

7. (Hold your head and say) I repossess my original head in the name of Jesus Christ.

8. Witchcraft operations on the day of my birth; die in the name of Jesus Christ.

³ And God said, Let there be light: and there was light.

9. Strange fires burning against my life; die in the name of Jesus Christ.

10. Light of God; illuminate my star now in the name of Jesus Christ.

11. By the light of the Lord, my star, my glory, shine by fire in the name of Jesus Christ.

12. Witchcraft pots, covering my head, scatter by fire in the name of Jesus Christ.

13. My star, my glory; shine beyond the veil of darkness in the name of Jesus Christ.

⁴ And God saw the light, that it was good: and God divided the light from the darkness.

- My destiny, jump out of darkness in the name of Jesus Christ.
- Satanic attachments between me and darkness, by the sword of fire, break and release me in the name of Jesus Christ.

⁵ And God called the light Day, and the darkness he called Night. And the evening and the morning were the first day.

14. Powers, turning my day into night, die by fire in the name of Jesus Christ.
15. Powers of the night, oppressing my destiny, die by fire in the name of Jesus Christ.
16. Powers, turning my glory to shame, die by fire in the name of Jesus Christ.

⁶ And God said, Let there be a firmament in the midst of the waters, and let it divide the waters from the waters.

17. Evil programming in the heavenly programmed against my joy, be aborted by fire in the name of Jesus Christ.

18. Forces drawing powers from the heavenly to waste my efforts, be struck by the thunder of God in the name of Jesus Christ.

19. My blessings suspended in the air, I pull you to myself now in the name of Jesus Christ.

20. Tokens of failures programmed into the north, into the south, into the east and into the west, against my testimonies, fail by fire in the name of Jesus Christ.

7 And God made the firmament, and divided the waters which were under the firmament from the waters which were above the firmament: and it was so. 8 And God called the firmament Heaven. And the evening and the morning were the second day.

21. Powers flying against my destiny; crash-land by fire in the name of Jesus Christ.

22. Covering cast above my destiny, sublime by fire in the name of Jesus Christ.

23. Heavens above my head; open by fire in the name of Jesus Christ.

24. My heavens, release the flood of my testimonies in the name of Jesus Christ.

⁹ And God said, Let the waters under the heaven be gathered together unto one place, and let the dry land appear: and it was so. 10 And God called the dry land Earth; and the gathering together of the waters called he Seas: and God saw that it was good.

- Rivers of delay standing before me, by the voice of the Lord, dry up now in the name of Jesus Christ.
- Oh Lord, make a way for me in the midst of my Red Sea in the name of Jesus Christ.
- Thou coast of my destiny, be enlarged by fire in the name of Jesus Christ.
- I shall not die in my Island of Patmos in the name of Jesus Christ.

¹¹ And God said, Let the earth bring forth grass, the herb yielding seed, and the fruit tree yielding fruit after his kind, whose seed is in itself, upon the earth: and it was so. 12 And the earth brought forth grass, and herb yielding seed after his kind, and the tree yielding fruit,

whose seed was in itself, after his kind: and God saw that it was good.
13 And the evening and the morning were the third day.

25. Leaves and roots assigned to injure my destiny, hear ye the word of the Lord; are you not the third day creation of my Father, lose your potency, catch fire in the name of Jesus Christ.

26. Powers of roots and herbs, working against my life, backfire by fire in the name of Jesus Christ.

27. Incantation-empowered herbs and roots, working against my life; be paralyzed by fire in the name of Jesus Christ.

14 And God said, Let there be lights in the firmament of the heaven to divide the day from the night; and let them be for signs, and for seasons, and for days, and years: 15 And let them be for lights in the firmament of the heaven to give light upon the earth: and it was so.

28. Powers, turning my journey of 40 minutes to 40 days, die by fire in the name of Jesus Christ.

29. My season of recovery, appear NOW by fire in the name of Jesus Christ.

30. Signs of rejection upon my life, I wipe you off by the blood of Jesus Christ.

16 And God made two great lights; the greater light to rule the day, and the lesser light to rule the night: he made the stars also. 17 And God set them in the firmament of the heaven to give light upon the earth, 18 And to rule over the day and over the night, and to divide the light from the darkness: and God saw that it was good. 19 And the evening and the morning were the fourth day.

- Anything programmed into the sun, the moon and stars to disturb my shining, catch fire in the name of Jesus Christ.
- I receive a rod of fire, I rule over my enemies in the name of Jesus Christ.
- My glory, shine for the whole world to see in the name of Jesus Christ.

20 And God said, Let the waters bring forth abundantly the moving creature that hath life, and fowl that may fly above the earth in the open firmament of heaven. 21 And God created great whales, and every living creature that moveth, which the waters brought forth abundantly, after their kind, and every winged fowl after his kind: and God saw that it was good. 22 And God blessed them, saying, Be fruitful, and multiply, and fill the waters in the seas, and let fowl multiply in the earth. 23 And the evening and the morning were the fifth day.

- Marine influence over my life, lose your hold in the name of Jesus Christ.

- Powers under water; on contract against my life, die in the name of Jesus Christ.

- My virtues buried underwater, by the power that floated the axe head in the days of Elisha, jump out by fire and locate me now in the name of Jesus Christ.

- Visitors from the waters; my life is no longer your candidate, die by fire in the name of Jesus Christ.

- Blood of Jesus Christ, pollute that body of water harbouring anything that belongs to me candidate in the name of Jesus Christ.

²⁴ And God said, Let the earth bring forth the living creature after his kind, cattle, and creeping thing, and beast of the earth after his kind: and it was so.

- Serpentine powers swallowing my blessings; vomit them by fire in the name of Jesus Christ.

- By the blood of Jesus Christ, covenants with serpentine powers, break and release me now.

²⁵ And God made the beast of the earth after his kind, and cattle after their kind, and every thing that creepeth upon the earth after his kind: and God saw that it was good.

- Household wickedness tormenting my life, collide with the Rock of Ages and die in the name of Jesus Christ.

- My portions in the hands of household enemies, I recover you by fire in the name of Jesus Christ.

- House witchcraft monitoring my life, receive total blindness in the name of Jesus Christ.

26 And God said, Let us make man in our image, after our likeness: and let them have dominion over the fish of the sea, and over the fowl of the air, and over the cattle, and over all the earth, and over every creeping thing that creepeth upon the earth.

- Negative anointing, working against my relevance; dry up by the voice of the Lord.
- I shall not pass through this earth like a shadow in the name of Jesus Christ.

27 So God created man in his own image, in the image of God created he him; male and female created he them. 28 And God blessed them, and God said unto them, Be fruitful, and multiply, and replenish the earth, and subdue it: and have dominion over the fish of the sea, and over the fowl of the air, and over every living thing that moveth upon the earth.

- By the help of heaven, I shall fulfil my purpose on earth in the name of Jesus Christ.
- I exercise dominion over my environments in the name of Jesus Christ.
- Authority of heaven, possess me now in the name of Jesus Christ.

- Staff of power, sword of divine justice; enter me now in the name of Jesus Christ.

29 And God said, Behold, I have given you every herb bearing seed, which is upon the face of all the earth, and every tree, in the which is the fruit of a tree yielding seed; to you it shall be for meat. 30 And to every beast of the earth, and to every fowl of the air, and to every thing that creepeth upon the earth, wherein there is life, I have given every green herb for meat: and it was so.

1. Blood of Jesus Christ, flush out poisons I ate and drank in dreams and in the physical in the name of Jesus Christ.

2. Rod of fire; crush the head of the serpent moving about in my body in the name of Jesus Christ.

3. I recover my staff of bread from the hands of oppressors in the name of Jesus Christ.

4. O Lord my Father, repair and restore my staff of bread in the name of Jesus Christ.

³¹ And God saw everything that he had made, and, behold, it was very good. And the evening and the morning were the sixth day.

- By fire, by fire, by fire, I shall reach my Promise Land in the name of Jesus Christ

- I reverse the truncation of my destiny in the name of Jesus Christ

- I get off diverted destination, Holy Ghost, put me back on track.

- My destiny is beautiful and very good in the name of Jesus Christ.

- Average! You are an enemy; get out of my life in the name of Jesus Christ

- By the power of the Holy Ghost, I am standing on the platform of excellence in the name of Jesus Christ

APPRECIATE THE LORD FOR PRAYERS ANSWERED.

MY FOUNDATIONS, BE REPAIRED BY FIRE!

...but the righteous is an everlasting foundation. Proverbs 10:25b

When refering to a structure, foundation is the platform upon which a building or structure is raised. If it is strong, the building or structure would be strong ; if it is weak, there may be cracks on the building. The building may even collapse.

Foundation could also mean the start point, the first time, the beginning, origin or source of a matter or person.

There are many foundations in the life of everyone. Ancestral foundations, marital foundations, academic foundations, spiritual foundations, etc.

If the foundations (not foundation) be destroyed, what can the righteous do? Psalms 11:3. Of course, he righteous has an option to rebuild and restructure his foundation – he/she should pray earnestly.

Prayer changes things.

TEXT:

Isaiah 58:12 54:11 1Kiings 7:10; Psalms11:3

CONFESSION:

…behold, (the Lord) will lay (my) stones with fair colours, and lay (my) foundations with sapphires.

SING PRAISES

PRAYER POINTS

1. My foundations; drink the blood of Jesus Christ.

2. Blood of Jesus Christ, speak mercy to my foundations.

3. Foundational sins, receive the atoning power of the blood of Jesus Christ

4. Foundational evil covenants, opening doors of affliction into my life, I break by the blood of Jesus Christ.

5. Yokes of foundational curse, break, in the name of Jesus Christ.

6. Foundational strongman attached to my life; die by fire, in the name of Jesus Christ.

7. My foundations, the blood of Jesus Christ is speaking to you, respond now.

8. Foundational evil covenants, opening doors of affliction into my life, break by the blood of Jesus Christ.

9. Evil foundational strongman, injecting sickness into my body and mind, fall down and die in the name of Jesus Christ.

10. Fire of God, deal with every root of misfortune in my foundation, in the name of Jesus Christ.

11. Destructive effects of polygamy in my foundations, be removed by the finger of God

12. Earthquake of the Lord, appear in my foundations in the name of Jesus Christ.

13. Stubborn covenants in my foundations, by the blood of Jesus Christ, break and release me now, in the name of Jesus Christ.

14. Witchcraft in my foundations; die by fire in the name of Jesus Christ.

15. Voices of the idols of my father's house and my mother's house, crying against my glory; by the voice of the Lord; be silent.

16. Affinity with the dead, by the blood of Jesus Christ, break by fire, in the name of Jesus Christ.

17. Residual evil affinity and attachments with my foundations and ancestral line; break by the blood of Jesus Christ.

18. Forces of darkness arrayed against my foundations, break and scatter by fire in the name of Jesus Christ.

19. Generational battles in my foundations; receive confusions, scatter by fire in the name of Jesus Christ.

20. Voices in my foundations saying 'Not so' to my help and helpers, the voice of the Lord silence you in the name of Jesus Christ.

21. Evil tongues in my foundations, disqualifying me as a candidate of divine help, by the authority of the Word of God, I condemn you in the name of Jesus Christ.

22. Forces of darkness in my foundations, chasing away helpers from me, die by fire in the name of Jesus Christ.

23. My foundations, receive the Holy Ghost fire in the name of Jesus Christ.

24. Light of God; disgrace the darkness in my foundations, in the name of Jesus Christ.

25. Evil foundational signatures of my ancestry; be erased from my life by the blood of Jesus Christ.

26. Foundational sins, affecting me negatively, by the blood of Jesus Christ, be washed away from my life.

27. Foundational evil transfers, dry up fire in the name of Jesus Christ.

28. Foundational evil patterns, catch fire in the name of Jesus Christ.

29. Carpenters of heaven, appear and repair the faults in my foundations in the name of Jesus Christ.

30. Evil flowing from foundations into my life through placenta, by the voice of the Lord, dry up now, in the name of Jesus Christ.

31. Mercy of the Lord, appear in my foundations, in the name of Jesus Christ.

32. Foundational affinity with water spirits; by the blood of Jesus Christ and the fire of the Holy Ghost, break and release me now.

33. Foundational evil dedication binding my life with spirit wife and spirit husband, by the blood of Jesus Christ, I renounce you, break by fire.

34. Parental and foundational curses, postponing my day of glory, I cancel you by the blood of Jesus Christ.

35. Blood of Jesus Christ, appear in my foundations, I need to move forward.

36. Awesome presence of God, swallow every foundational influence, redeploying my expectations in the name of Jesus Christ.

37. Serpents and scorpions of darkness in my foundations, I crush your head in the name of Jesus Christ.

38. Finger of God, appear and repair the faults and cracks in my foundations.

39. Weak foundations, not strong enough to carry my destiny; be replaced by fire.

40. My foundations; arise and praise the Lord in the name of Jesus Christ.

APPRECIATE THE LORD FOR PRAYERS ANSWERED

PRAYER TO CONCEIVE OUTSTANDING IDEAS

....for that which is conceived in her is of the Holy Ghost. Mat 1:20b

Divine pregnancy means uncommon ideas, new inventions, rare innovations, wisdom that profits, etc. History shows that great people like Michael Faradays, the inventor of electricity, Isaac Newton, the discoverer of the Law of Gravity, Johann Kepler, father of physical astronomy, Blaise Pascal, father of hydrostatics, etc., are all Christians.

Inventors are celebrities, and celebrated; innovators are rewarded.

How Do Divine Ideas Come?

a. Through constant meditation of the word of God

b. Having a time alone for silent moments daily (could be daytime or nighttime).

c. Natural gifting. 1Sa10:6

d. by honing your talents

e.   Searching for profits along the line of your God given talent/s

f.   Constant studying of the Bible

g.   Spending night time to ponder and find solutions to knotty challenges

h.   Always finding solutions to challenges of life; not running away from it

i.   Through anointing impartation. 1Sa10:6

Pray now to unleash that giant, that greatness in you.

TEXT:

Matthew 25:15 – 23; 1John 2:27; Deuteronomy 8:18,

CONFESSION:

And the Spirit of the LORD will come upon (me)..., and shalt be turned into another man. 1Samuel 10:6

SING PRAISES

PRAYER POINTS

1.   (Hold your head) My head, my brain, swim in the blood of Jesus Christ

2.   Blood of Jesus Christ, purge my brain.

3.   Arrows of memory failures, fired at my brain, back fire by fire.

4.   Programming of brain fog, I shake you out of my head by fire in the name of Jesus Christ

5.   My head, my head, reject bewitchment in the name of Jesus Christ

6.   My brain, my brain, jump out of witchcraft cauldron in the name of Jesus Christ

7.   I receive eyes of Elijah, I receive the ear of Samuel in the name of Jesus Christ

8.   My gifts and talents, jump out of witchcraft grave in the name of Jesus Christ

9.   My cutting-edge ideas, my innovations, my invention, receive divine attention in the name of Jesus Christ.

10.   Creative power of the Holy Ghost, enter me now in the name of Jesus Christ

11.   Seed of procrastination in me, die by fire in the name of Jesus Christ

12.   Evil hands on my head, wither by fire in the name of Jesus Christ

13.   Holy Ghost, overshadow my head in the name of Jesus Christ

14.   Oh Lord, make me a mysterious wonder in the name of Jesus Christ

15. Spirit of the Lord move over the face of my thoughts in the name of Jesus Christ

16. Anointing for rare innovations, fall upon me in the name of Jesus Christ

17. Anointing for uncommon ideas, fall upon me in the name of Jesus Christ

18. I would not labour for another man to eat in the name of Jesus Christ

19. My brain, conceive uncommon ideas and lucrative initiatives

20. Oh Lord my Father, show me the pot oil in my possession in the name of Jesus Christ

21. I see water in the desert, I see highway in the wilderness in the name of Jesus Christ

22. I see gold in mud, I see honey in carcasses in the name of Jesus Christ

23. Light of the Lord, possess my brain in the name of Jesus Christ

24. Anointing to be a carrier of solution, possess me now in the name of Jesus Christ

25. Wisdom to be wiser than the ancient, possess me now.

I RECOVER MY COATS OF MANY COLOURS

And God saw everything that he had made, and, behold, it was very good. Gen 1:31

Everyone's destiny on earth is originally created beautiful. And like Joseph's father, God the Father gave every destiny a coat of many colours.

Household wickedness are the primary thieves of coat of many colours. *And it came to pass, when Joseph was come unto his brethren, that they stript Joseph out of his coat, his coat of many colours that was on him;* Genesis 37:23

If you are not living up to your potential, and there is nothing really attractive or enviable about your life, it means your coat of many colours has been stolen or lost. Then you need to recover it.

Gen_37:3 Now Israel loved Joseph more than all his children, because he was the son of his old age: and he made him a coat of many colours.

TEXT:

Genesis 37:23, 32; 1:31; John 3:35,

CONFESSION:

I will praise thee; for I am fearfully and wonderfully made: marvellous are thy works; and that my soul knoweth right well. Psalms 139:14

SING PRAISES

PRAYER POINTS

1. Mercy that brings recovery, locate me by the blood of Jesus Christ

2. Foundational covenants, empowering household wickedness to steal from me, break by the blood of Jesus Christ.

3. Blood covenants, empowering spirit spouse to steal from me, break by the blood of Jesus Christ.

4. Anointing to pray and prevail, possess me now in the name of Jesus Christ.

5. Spirit wife, spirit husband stealing from me, die by fire

6. Household wickedness, stealing from me, be arrested by fire; return my property now in the name of Jesus Christ.

7. I pursue the thieves of my destiny, I overtake them, I recover all my stolen glories in the name of Jesus Christ.

8. Anything in me that is not of God, die by fire in the name of Jesus Christ.

9. Light of the Lord, expose and disgrace unfriendly friends in the name of Jesus Christ.

10. Sworn enemies of my father's house, die by fire in the name of Jesus Christ.

11. My feet, carry me away from where evil awaits me in the name of Jesus Christ.

12. I jump out of witchcraft well in which household enemies had thrown me into the name of Jesus Christ.

13. Household wickedness, chasing me into the wilderness, your time is over, die by fire in the name of Jesus Christ.

14. Like unto the enemies of King Jehoshaphat, confusion from the Lord enter into the midst of household wickedness and external enemies of my soul in the name of Jesus Christ.

15. I withdraw the control of my life from the hands and domination of the household wickedness in the name of Jesus Christ.

16. I release my future from the influence and control of the household wickedness in the name of Jesus Christ.

17. Let the terrible fire of God; consume the transportation system of my household witchcraft in the name of Jesus Christ.

18. Every agent, ministering at the altar of witchcraft in my household, fall down and die in the name of Jesus Christ.

19. Let the thunder and fire of God, locate the storehouse and strong-room of my household witchcraft harbouring my blessings and pull them down, in the name of Jesus Christ.

20. Every decision, vow, and covenant of household witchcraft affecting me be nullified by the blood of Jesus

21. I send confusion into the camp of household witchcraft, in the name of Jesus Christ.

22. Right arm of the Lord, lift me up from the prison to the palace in the name of Jesus Christ.

23. Long time lies against me, be exposed by fire, in the name of Jesus Christ.

24. By fire, by fire, by fire, I recover my coats of many colours and all the profits made with it; in the name of Jesus Christ.

THANK YOU JESUS! THANK YOU JESUS!! THANK YOU
JESUS!!!

RECOVERY FROM DESTINY MANIPULATION

And the Spirit of God was hovering…. Gen 1:2b

There is no bad destiny; there may only be manipulated destiny. Destiny first got hijacked in the Garden of Eden. Serpent's trick in the Garden is one of the ways of witchcraft – manipulation and machination.

Everyone and everything; you and I; and all other things that God created were made very good. Genesis 1:31. There were no problems, no trouble, no bondage, no sickness, no trauma; everything was just wonderful, excellent, beautiful, perfect, etc., until the manipulation.

You are not an error on earth. You were created to shine and be fulfilled. You can reverse that manipulation.

TEXT:
Revelation 4:11; Genesis 1:2-4; Psalms 92:4-5,

CONFESSION:

I will praise thee; for I am fearfully and wonderfully made: marvellous are thy works; and that my soul knoweth right well. Psa139:14

SING PRAISES

PRAYER POINTS

1. Spirit of God! Come upon me now, in the name of Jesus Christ.

2. Witchcraft manipulation of my destiny, expire by fire, in the name of Jesus Christ.

3. Spirit of God, incubate my destiny now, in the name of Jesus.

4. Generational curses; manipulating the seeds of my lineage; break by fire in the name of Jesus Christ.

5. Holy Ghost fire, overshadow me now, in the name of Jesus.

6. Satanic twist of my destiny; be reversed by fire in the name of Jesus Christ.

7. Voice of the Lord, possess my voice, in the name of Jesus.

8. Powers in my roots troubling my destiny, die by fire in the name of Jesus.

9. Blood of Jesus Christ, paralyze every ritual assigned to paralyze my destiny

10. My destiny; jump out of witchcraft graves in the name of Jesus Christ.

11. Presence of the Lord, possess my essence in the name of Jesus Christ.

...the earth was without form: Genesis 1:3a

This means a twist or a manipulation from the original form, or there is no definite shape.

Some lives are indeed in disarray, no shape, fragmented, unattractive, ugly-looking, mixed-up, nothing meaningful to show for being alive, no reason for continuing living, etc.

Please pray these prayers aggressively:

12. Carpenters of heaven; descend and repair my destiny; in the name of Jesus Christ.

13. You my life, before you finish this prayer, receive a glorious shape in the name of Jesus Christ.

14. Placental manipulation of my life, be reversed by the blood Jesus Christ.

15. You my life, before you leave this program, be filled with glorious things in the name of Jesus Christ.

16. Fragmented parts of my life, by the finger of God, be re-arranged by fire in the name of Jesus Christ.

17. Witchcraft powers that had tampered with my destiny, your time is up, die by fire in the name of Jesus Christ.

18. Right arm of the Lord, appear now and repair my life by fire in the name of Jesus Christ.

...the earth was void... (a life is void when it is empty, no contents, no value, desolate, no back-up, no helper/help, feels abandoned):

At the moment, everything looks just empty - empty pockets, empty account, life empty of testimonies, empty house - (no spouse, no child), empty brain, empty shop/workshop, etc.

The in-coming months are non-promising; nothing meaningful to pursue - the future looks unsure and bleak. At times, you see yourselves as useless. You see no value for your existence. At some time, you asked, "Why I am still alive?"

You have been called good-for-nothing and you see yourself as so. No, you are not good-for-nothing.

Why does your life seem empty? Why does the year itself look empty; nothing promising about it?

It is because some things which once filled that life have been stolen. Who stole them?

Who stole them? Recover them this way:

19. O earth, O earth, O earth, as you fought for Moses, this morning, fight for me too.

20. Flying roll of fire, arrest and destroy every spiritual robber stealing from my destiny.

21. Spiritual robbers, stealing from me, die.

22. Household witchcraft, stealing from good things from my life, die by fire in the name of Jesus Christ.

23. My captured destiny in the custody of marine witchcraft, receive deliverance by fire in the name of Jesus Christ.

24. Foundational witchcraft, stealing from good things from my life, die by fire in the name of Jesus Christ.

25. I recover every virtue pressed out of me in my sleep by fire in the name of Jesus Christ.

26. By fire, by fire, I enter into labour, I abort all evil strangers residing in my body/spirit in the name of Jesus Christ.

27. By fire, by fire, I recover, every missed opportunity in my life in the name of Jesus Christ.

28. Glory of God, saturate my life by fire in the name of Jesus Christ.

29. Beauty of heaven; cover me all over in the name of Jesus Christ.

30. Oh Lord, make my life like the Garden of Eden once again in the name of Jesus Christ.

31. By the mercy of God, you my stolen glory, you my stolen star, be restored by fire in the name of Jesus Christ.

... and darkness was upon the face of the deep...

Darkness signifies no sense of direction, complete confusion, feeling lost, presence of elements or agents of darkness in a life, no vision (spiritual or mental), being ignorant of one's problem or the origin of the problem.

Prophesy forth into your life thus:

32. Presence of darkness, around my life, in my life, upon my life; be disgraced by the light of God in the name of Jesus Christ.

33. Agents of darkness, operating in my life, die by fire in the name of Jesus Christ.

34. Elemental forced operating against my greatness, die by fire in the name of Jesus Christ.

35. Instruments of darkness, installed against my life, scatter by fire in the name of Jesus Christ.

36. Light of God, appear and disgrace every presence of darkness covering my essence in the name of Jesus Christ.

37. Arrow of confusion, programmed against me this year, I fire you back in the name of Jesus Christ.

38. Visions of transformation, my life is available, enter me in the name of Jesus Christ.

39. Visions of regeneration, my life is available, enter me in the name of Jesus Christ.

40. Visions of restoration, my life is available, enter me in the name of Jesus Christ.

41. Fragmented parts of my life, by the Spirit of God, gather yourselves together now and be made whole.

42. Resurrection power in the Spirit of God, bring my dead back to life in the name of Jesus Christ.

43. Error in my destiny, receive divine correction in the name of Jesus Christ.

44. Thou Spirit of God, descend now, and renew my destiny in the name of Jesus Christ.

DELIVERANCE FROM WITCHCRAFT SUPPRESSION

To execute upon them the judgment written:... Psalms 149:9

Pressed down in your sleep? or there was an unusual or suspicious goose-bumps feelings, or you feel light-headed? Was there a time you got caught in a swirling wind for up to 4 seconds? You never know, it might be that a diabolical entity is programmed into that wind. That satanic entity or deposit is meant to drop in the life of the targeted victim.

When you are pressed down in sleep, either or both of these might have happened to you.

a. Virtues pressed out of you. E.g. approaching opportunities, promotion, innovations, success, privilege, help, lifting or/and seed of the womb.

Other virtues pressed out could be spiritual entities like zeal for God's service, vibrant prayer life, ardent word study life, burden for evangelism, etc.

It's time to recollect them.

b. Dark deposits pressed into you

Such deposits could be sickness, stones at the mouth of the womb, strange objects in the brain, marks of rejection or hatred for no reasons, internal heat or poison in the scrotal sacs, evil odour, seed of rejection, failure or setbacks, heaviness in the spirit, laziness in prayer life, slow speed in life, holes in the hands, etc.

It's time to eject them.

TEXT:

Job 4:14

14 Fear came upon me, and trembling, Which made all my bones shake. 15 Then a spirit passed before my face; The hair on my body stood up. 16 It stood still, But I could not discern its appearance. A form was before my eyes; There was silence; Then I heard a voice saying.

CONFESSION:

[1] He who dwells in the secret place of the Most High Shall abide under the shadow of the Almighty. [2] I will say of the Lord, "He is my refuge and my fortress; My God, in Him I will trust." [3] Surely He shall deliver you from the snare of the fowler And from the perilous pestilence. [4] He shall cover you with His feathers, And under His wings you shall take refuge; His truth shall be your shield and buckler. [5] You shall not be afraid of the terror by night, Nor of the arrow that flies by day, [6] Nor of the pestilence that walks in darkness, Nor of the destruction that lays waste at noonday. Psalms 91:1-6 (NKJV)

SING PRAISES

PRAYER POINTS

1. Blood of Jesus Christ, wash away the sins in my life.

2. Sins in my life, unrighteousness in my being, opening doors to demonic attacks, by the blood of Jesus Christ, be washed away.

3. Blood of Jesus Christ, avail for me now.

4. *(Say this severally)* I swallow the Holy Ghost fire, I drink the blood of Jesus Christ

5. Witchcraft pressed-in into my body, soul and spirit, jump out by fire in the name of Jesus Christ.

6. Satanic deposits into my body, soul and spirit, catch fire in the name of Jesus Christ.

7. Right arm of the Lord, uproot occult plantation pressed into my body, soul and spirit, in the name of Jesus Christ.

8. West wind of God, blow back the virtues pressed out of my body, soul and spirit in the name of Jesus Christ.

9. Every opening to witchcraft attacks in my life, by the key of David, be shut by fire, be shut forever in the name of Jesus Christ.

10. Thunder of God, visit witchcraft structures in my environment, and scatter them onto desolation in the name of Jesus Christ

11. *(Say this severally)*, I swallow the Holy Ghost fire, I drink the blood of Jesus Christ.

12. Witchcraft hands that is pressing me down; like the hand of Jeroboam the son of Nebat, wither by fire in the name of Jesus Christ

13. Right arm of the Lord, possess my hands in the name of Jesus Christ.

(Demonstrate the following prayer points)

14. Witchcraft press-in of .... into my body, soul and spirit, by the right arm of the Lord, be uprooted by fire in the name of Jesus Christ.

{failures, near-success, prayerlessness, uncleanness, sickness, infirmities, demotion, errors, incurable diseases, stagnation, evil marks, misconduct, miscarriage, heaviness in the spirit, (*mention more*)}

15. Witchcraft hands pressing and suppressing me, by the sword of fire, I cut you off in the name of Jesus Christ.

16. By the right arm of the Lord, I recover .... pressed out of me in the name of Jesus Christ.

good success prayerfulness   holiness   healing

promotion   excellence   advancement divine marks

greatness   spiritual agility

spiritual sensitivity   revelation knowledge   fresh oil

grace that brings favour   glory that beautifies,

(*mention more as it relates to your matter*)

17. Awesome presence of the Lord, tabernacle upon me and my household in the name of Jesus Christ.

(GIVE THE LORD WAVE OFFERINGS FOR PRAYERS ANSWERED)

PRAYER TO RECOVER LOST GLORY

...he shall restore double. Exodus 22:4b

You dreamed of losing or misplacing your luggage, an item or an opportunity? Or part of your hair or beard been shaved by unknown hands? Have you been robbed of a right or honour, promotion, possession or denied a privilege?

Or you lost a position due to behavioural shortfalls like taking a hasty decision, indecision, thoughtless carelessness, etc.

Mercy of God can still reinstate you.

TEXT:

Isaiah 52:3-6; 45:13; 49:24; Joel 2:25; Genesis 40:13

CONFESSION:

And (the Lord) will restore to (me) the years that the locust hath eaten, the cankerworm, and the caterpiller, and the palmerworm, (His) great army which I(He) sent among (us). Joel 2:25

SING PRAISES

PRAYER POINTS

(The following prayer is to be prayed with holy annoyance and with the spirit of enough-is-enough)

(*Prayer 1 – 5 should be prayed on your knees*).

1. Oh Lord, I plead for mercy – forgive me in any way I have sold myself out.

2. Blood of Jesus Christ speak mercy into my life; speak redemption into my life.

3. Voice of the Lord in the blood of Jesus Christ, plead for my redemption now before the court of heaven.

4. Mercy of God, avail for me in this prayer in the name of Jesus Christ.

5. Voice of the Lord in the blood of Jesus Christ, tell the captors of my virtues, glory and star that my redemption is now.

6. By the blood of Jesus Christ, I buy back my lost virtues, glory and stars in the name of Jesus Christ.

7. Ungodly covenants between me and the captors of my virtues and portions, by the blood of Jesus Christ, break and release me.

8. Blood and bloodless covenants between me and the captors of my virtues and portions, by the blood of Jesus Christ, break and release me.

9. Lawful captivity of my virtues, glory and stars; I revoke you all by the blood of Jesus Christ.

10. Lawful claims of the captors of my virtues, rights, privileges and portions, by the blood of Jesus Christ, I declare you null and void.

11. Star killers, glory killers, die by fire in the name of Jesus Christ

12. Fire of God, roast every chain tying down my virtues, glory, promotion and star in the name of Jesus Christ.

13. (Shout) JESUS CHRIST! Your death for my redemption on the cross of Calvary cannot be in vain – in your mercy and power, redeem my lost glory for me.

14. Captors of my glory, honour and virtues, by the authority in the name of Jesus Christ, release them by fire in the name of Jesus Christ.

15. After the order of Goliath, you the strongman, guarding the strong room and the warehouse where my virtues, privileges and portions are kept, fall down and die in the name of Jesus Christ.

16. I enter into the strong room and the warehouse of the captors of my virtues, I recover my portions and greatness in the name of Jesus Christ.

17. Captors of my virtues, lifting and portions, release me and die by fire in the name of Jesus Christ

18. By fire, by fire, by fire, I recover my lost virtues, glory, stars and portions in the name of Jesus Christ.

19. My Father and my Help, heal my portions in the name of Jesus Christ

20. By the authority of heaven, I claim every profit made with my stolen virtues, glory and stars, in the name of Jesus Christ.

21. I shut the door and the gate of my life to the plunderers and captors of portions and stars in the name of Jesus Christ.

GIVE THANKS TO GOD FOR THE RECOVERY OF YOUR VIRTUES, GLORY, STAR, PRIVILEGES, RIGHTS, PROMOTION AND PORTIONS.

BREAKING PARENTAL CURSES

Christ hath redeemed us from the curse of the law... Gal 3:13a

Any pronouncement a parent made upon his/her child is potent and binding upon a child, be it good or evil – except if it is not justified. (Proverbs 26:2).

Noah pronounced a curse on his son Ham. Jacob made negative pronouncements on three of his sons Reuben, Simeon and Levi – all these came to pass on these sons.

Mercy of God is available to you, to repair your destiny truncated by the curses of your parents.

TEXT:

Psalms 29:4-8, Ephesians 1:7, Hebrew 12:24; Gen 9:20-25

CONFESSION:

Christ hath redeemed us from the curse of the law, being made a curse for us: for it is written, Cursed is every one that hangeth on a tree: That the blessing of Abraham might come on the Gentiles through Jesus Christ; that we might receive the promise of the Spirit through faith. Gal 3:13 -14

SING PRAISES

PRAYER POINTS

1. Voice of the blood of Jesus Christ, speak mercy for me. (*Repeat this prayer several times until you hear the voice of the Holy Spirit say, Enough*).

2. Mercy of God, appear to me in this prayer in the name of Jesus Christ.

3. Voice of the blood of Jesus Christ, contend and silence every voice crying against my glory.

4. Curses of the forefathers, raging in my life, by the blood of Jesus Christ, break and release me.

5. Legal ground of curses in my roots, receive the blood of Jesus Christ.

6. Legal ground of curses in my destiny, receive the blood of Jesus Christ.

7. Negative pronouncements from the mouth of my grandfather upon my father, by the blood of Jesus Christ, break and release me.

8. Negative pronouncements from the mouth of my father upon my life, by the blood of Jesus Christ, break and release me.

9. Negative pronouncements from the mouth of my grandmother upon my mother, by the blood of Jesus Christ, break and release me.

10. Negative pronouncements from the mouth of my mother upon my life, by the blood of Jesus Christ, break and release me.

11. Parental spell pronounced on my head in my sleep, sublime by fire in the name of Jesus Christ.

12. Negative parental pronouncement uttered into my life, while I was in the blood of my birth, sublime by fire in the name of Jesus Christ.

13. Rage of jinx in my life, break and scatter in the name of Jesus Christ.

14. Strongman of affliction set in motion by parental curses to trouble my greatness, fall down and die, fire in the name of Jesus Christ.

15. Cycle of stagnancy, moulded by parental curses, by the hammer of fire, break and release me in the name of Jesus Christ.

16. Cycle of stagnancy, reinforced by parental curses, by the hammer of fire, break and release me in the name of Jesus Christ.

17. Altar of barrenness, established by parental evil pronouncement, by the hammer of fire, scatter in the name of Jesus Christ.

18. Barriers of limitation, erected by parental evil pronouncement, by the hammer of fire, scatter in the name of Jesus Christ.

19. Every ground I have lost because of parental curses, I recover you by mercy and fire in the name of Jesus Christ.

20. Contrariness in my destiny, be overturned by mercy and the fire of the Holy Ghost in the name of Jesus Christ.

21. My glory covered by the dross of parental curses, receive the washing of the blood of Jesus Christ.

22. I am delivered by fire, my glory, arise, and shine in the name of Jesus Christ.

23. Thou sun of my destiny that had set, wherever you are, arise, shine in the name of Jesus Christ.

24. I recover by fire, all my wasted years in the name of Jesus Christ.

25. Voice of the Lord, pronounce me blessed in the name of Jesus Christ.

26. Brand new blessed me, begin to march forward.

(GIVE THANKS AND WORSHIP THE LORD FOR PRAYERS ANSWERED)

40 PRAYER BULLETS TO EXIT FROM THE WILDERNESS

Thou shalt no more be termed Forsaken… Isaiah 62:4

Wilderness, *Hebrew "jeshimon", "a desert waste; Hebrew "tohu",* *"desolate place", a place of "waste" or "unoccupied"* a place *"without form".* Deuteronomy 32:10.

It is a dry land or desert; abandoned, forsaken, barren place or situation. It is a land without lanes, paths, routes or direction – a life without meaning, form or shape. It is a life devoid of planning because there is nothing to plan on.

But here is one of God's promises for you; *Thou shalt no more be termed Forsaken; neither shall thy land anymore be termed Desolate: but thou shalt be called Hephzibah, and thy land Beulah: for the LORD delighteth in thee, and thy land shall be married. Isa 62:4*

TEXT:

Acts 7:36; Isaiah 43:19; Lamentation 3 :2; Jeremiah 31:2; 3 John 1:2

CONFESSION:

(I) shall no more be termed Forsaken; neither shall (my) land anymore be termed Desolate: but (I) shall be called Hephzibah, and (my) land Beulah: for the LORD delights in (me), and (my) land shall be married. Isaiah 62:4

SING PRAISES

PRAYER POINTS

1. Mercy of the Lord; avail for me in this prayer in the name of Jesus Christ.

2. Ancestral sins, parental sins, personal sins keeping me in the wilderness of life, receive the atoning power of the blood of Jesus Christ.

3. Ancestral curses, parental curses, personal curses keeping me in the wilderness of life, receive the neutralising power of the blood of Jesus Christ.

4. Ancestral covenants, personal covenants keeping me in the wilderness of life, receive the dissolving power of the blood of Jesus Christ

5. Unconscious and conscious covenants with hardship; break by the blood of Jesus Christ, break by fire.

6. I break out of the cage of ignorance keeping me in the valley and in the wilderness in the name of Jesus Christ.

7. By the blood of Jesus Christ, break by the fire of the Holy Ghost; covenant with poverty, break and release me now.

8. I have stayed long enough in this wilderness, mercy of God, right arm of the Lord, walk me out in the name of Jesus Christ.

   (Double your aggression for the following prayer points)

9. By fire, by fire, by fire, wilderness of poverty die; in the name of Jesus Christ.

10. By fire, by fire, by fire, wilderness of barrenness die; in the name of Jesus Christ.

11. By fire, by fire, by fire, wilderness of demotion die; in the name of Jesus Christ.

12. By fire, by fire, by fire, wilderness of sickness die; in the name of Jesus Christ.

13. By fire, by fire, by fire, wilderness of dishonour die; in the name of Jesus Christ.

14. By fire, by fire, by fire, wilderness of stagnancy die; in the name of Jesus Christ.

15. Oh God of Abraham, promote me above my adversaries, in the name of Jesus Christ.

16. O God, arise and convert my poverty to prosperity today, in the name of Jesus Christ.

17. By the thunder of God, I contend with the spirit of poverty and I prevail, in the name of Jesus Christ.

18. My hands; refuse to befriend poverty, in the name of Jesus Christ.

19. Rivers of blessing in my life shall not dry, in the name of Jesus Christ.

20. Any power hiding my key of elevation, release it and die, in the name of Jesus Christ.

21. Angels of the Living God, prepare special fire for poverty in my life, in the name of Jesus Christ.

22. You the Egyptians, chasing me into the wilderness, turn back and die, in the name of Jesus Christ.

23. Household wickedness, chasing me into the wilderness, your time is over, die by fire in the name of Jesus Christ.

24. Character disorder prolonging my stay in the wilderness of life, die by fire in the name of Jesus Christ.

25. Witchcraft pronouncement prolonging my stay in the wilderness of hardship, by the voice of the Lord; be silent now.

26. Satanic remote control working against my speed in life, catch fire in the name of Jesus Christ.

27. Odour of rejection on my personality; be washed away by the blood of Jesus Christ.

28. I reject every re-invitation to the arena of poverty, in the name of Jesus Christ.

29. Storms of wilderness, by the voice of the Lord, Peace be still, in the name of Jesus Christ.

30. Ancestral evil agreements with poverty, binding upon my life, be revoked by the blood of Jesus Christ.

31. Thou serpent of poverty in my life, be buried alive in the name of Jesus Christ.

32. Cycle of poverty in my family, break by fire, in the name of Jesus

33. Bondage of slavery, catch fire in the name of Jesus Christ.

34. Chain of oppression, be roasted by fire in the name of Jesus Christ

35. By fire, by fire, by fire, I move from wilderness of poverty to evergreen of prosperity; in the name of Jesus Christ.

36. By fire, by fire, by fire, I move from wilderness of barrenness to status of fruitfulness; in the name of Jesus Christ.

37. By fire, by fire, by fire, I move from wilderness of demotion to platform of promotions; in the name of Jesus Christ.

38. By fire, by fire, by fire, I move from wilderness of sickness to the land of wellness; in the name of Jesus Christ.

39. By fire, by fire, by fire, I move from wilderness of dishonour to the castle of indescribable honour; in the name of Jesus

40. By fire, by fire, by fire, I move from wilderness of stagnancy into the vehicle of divine speed; in the name of Jesus Christ.

NOTE:

Prosperity don't just answer to prayers but to prayers and giving. So, sow a sacrificial seed immediately after praying this prayer towards this vision, to your Pastor's life, unto any poor in the midst of your church or to a poor neighbour.

GIVE THANKS AND WORSHIP THE LORD FOR PRAYERS ANSWERED

PRAYER FOR PERSONAL REVIVAL

Wilt thou not revive us again: that thy people may rejoice in thee?

Psalms 85:6

Fire on your prayer altar is dim; you are no more delighted when you hear, 'Let's go to house of the Lord'. Evangelism excitement has become, 'Once upon a time.' You are no more consumed by the 'zeal of my Father's house.'

You are too heavy to wake up in the night. It's easier to talk for hours but hectic to pray for minutes. Personal Bible study has become once in a blue moon.

Arise from your ashes, pray and you shall be revived again. '...*Be of good comfort, rise; he calleth thee.'* Mark 10:49.

Be on fire again.

TEXT:

Psalms 138:7; 80:18; *Acts 3:19*

CONFESSION:

:¹⁰ Create in me a clean heart, O God; and renew a right spirit within me. ¹¹ Cast me not away from thy presence; and take not thy holy spirit from me. ¹² Restore unto me the joy of thy salvation; and uphold me with thy free spirit. Psalms 51:10 -12

SING PRAISES

PRAYER POINTS

1. God of love, God of mercy, You are my Father, pardon all my sins, overlook my iniquities, shortcomings, trespasses and transgressions in the name of Jesus Christ.

2. Fountain of the blood of Jesus Christ, wash away the stains and the stench of my sins.

3. Repercussions of sins in my life, building a gulf between me and my Maker, be removed by the mercy of God.

4. Residual evil affinity and attachments with my foundations and ancestral line, break by the blood of Jesus Christ.

5. Every dross in my spirit-man, catch fire in the name of Jesus Christ.

6. Dark spot upon my spiritual garment, be cleansed by the blood of Jesus Christ.

7. Negative voices in me, calling my God a liar, shut up in the name of Jesus Christ.

8. Negative forces around me, calling my God a liar, be paralysed by fire in the name of Jesus Christ.

1. NOTE:

2. *If you pray 9 – 13 with an undivided attention, there will be some minor manifestations like, yawning, tears flowing from the eyes, nose discharge, farting, phlegm in the throat, etc., keep praying, don't even pause.]*

9. *[Demonstrate this; say 21 times]* I swallow the Holy Ghost fire; I drink the blood of Jesus Christ.

10. *[Lay your right hand on your stomach and breathe heavily]* Witchcraft food eaten in my dream to weaken my sprit-man, be flushed out by the blood of Jesus Christ.

11. Deposit of sex in dreams, weakening my spiritual agility, die by fire in the name of Jesus Christ.

12. Magnet of sin in my flesh and mind, catch fire in the name of Jesus Christ.

13. Demons of lust, feasting through my eyes, jump out, die by fire

14. Ancestral evil flow into my life, by the voice of the Lord, dry up now in the name of Jesus Christ.

15. Ancestral evil resemblance in my life, cease by fire in the name of Jesus Christ.

16. Anointing of like father like son; like mother like daughter, my case is different, die by fire in the name of Jesus Christ.

17. Unpleasant past experiences sponsoring discouragement and depression, by the blood of Jesus Christ, be erased from my mind.

18. Unfriendly friends, ungodly friends, dragging me down spiritually, depart from my life by fire.

19. Unfriendly friends, ungodly friends, pulling me away from my Maker, depart from me by fire.

20. Unfriendly friends, ungodly friends, dragging me down in any aspect of life, depart from my life by fire.

21. Purging fire of God, enter me in the name of Jesus Christ.

22. Every pollution, every dross causing weakness in my spirit-man, catch fire in the name of Jesus Christ.

23. Revival fire, enter me now and purge me in the name of Jesus Christ.

24. Revival fire, enter me now and re-vitalize my spirit-man in the name of Jesus Christ.

25. Evil food eaten in dreams and in the physical, that is now crippling my spiritual life, be flushed out blood of Jesus Christ.

26. Evil food eaten in dreams and in the physical, causing spiritual dizziness and laziness, be purged out by the blood of Jesus Christ.

27. Covenants from illicit sex, affecting my spiritual life, break by the blood of Jesus Christ.

28. Voice of the Lord in the blood of Jesus Christ, speak pardon, speak resurrection into my spirit in the name of Jesus Christ.

3. [*Say the following severally and aggressively*]

29. I receive the Holy Ghost fire, I become fire, I release fire in the name of Jesus Christ.

30. Anointing of God that cannot be insulted, enter me now in the name of Jesus Christ.

31. Energising fire of God, enter me in the name of Jesus Christ.

32. Fortifying fire of God, enter me and sustain me the name of Jesus Christ.

33. Seed of backsliding in me die by fire in the name of Jesus Christ.

34. Seed of laziness in studying the word of God, die by fire in the name of Jesus Christ.

35. Distractions and delusions preventing me from studying the scriptures, clear away by fire in the name of Jesus Christ.

36. Diversions and deviations preventing me from studying the scriptures, clear away by fire in the name of Jesus Christ.

37. East wind of God, blow away satanic mist and cyst preventing me from understanding and assimilating the Word.

38. My inner-man, receive fire, my inner-man become fire, my inner-man release fire in the name of Jesus Christ.

39. By the blood of Jesus Christ, I reverse every spiritual burial conducted for my finances.

40. Covenant with poverty break by fire in the name of Jesus Christ.

41. By the key of David, I open the doors to my financial freedom in the name of Jesus Christ.

42. My flesh, bones and blood, receive fire, become too for affliction in the name of Jesus Christ.

43. My body, reject bewitchment in the name of Jesus Christ.

44. Fire of healing and health, surge through my body in the name of Jesus Christ.

45. Mighty hand of God, pull partial or complete backsliding out of me in the name of Jesus Christ.

46. Strength of God, strength from God, strength in God, envelope my spirit, soul and body in the name of Jesus Christ.

47. Right arm of the Lord, hold me in my walk with the Lord in the name of Jesus Christ.

48. [*Shout*] Jesus Christ! Hold me tight, I want to keep walking with You.

WORSHIP THE LORD FOR PRAYER ANSWERED

HOLY GHOST, IGNITE MY FIRE!

...he shall baptize you with the Holy Ghost, and with fire: Mat 3:11

And Jesus said, … I perceive that virtue is gone out of me. Luke 8:46

According to a song writer;

Breathe on me *2ce*

Holy Ghost fire,

Breathe on me

YESTERDAY IS GONE,

Today I'm in need, of Holy Ghost fire

Breathe on me

God's fire in us; His anointing upon our lives, needs to be rekindle, and be refilled, and be re-fired, over and over and over again.

And when he had sent them away, he departed into a mountain to pray (to get refilled). Mark 6:46

TEXT:

Acts 2 :1 - 4; 1: 4 - 5; Matthew 3 :11; Isaiah 11:2-3

CONFESSION:

And the spirit of the LORD shall rest upon (me), the spirit of wisdom and understanding, the spirit of counsel and might, the spirit of knowledge and of the fear of the LORD; Isaiah 11:2

SING PRAISES 20 minutes

PRAYER POINTS

1. Blood of Jesus Christ, purge me of spiritual pollutions.

2. Spiritual contaminations blocking more of God in me, be flushed out by the blood of Jesus Christ.

3. Hindrances to the free flow of God's fire in me, receive divine flushing in the name of Jesus Christ.

4. Every clog in the wheel of my anointing, roast by fire in the name of Jesus Christ

5. Dross of spiritual sluggishness receive heavenly lubricants, loose in the name of Jesus Christ.

6. Blockages in my spiritual pipes, I shake you off by fire in the name of Jesus Christ.

7. Like on the day of Pentecost in the upper room, wind and fire, enter me now, in the name of Jesus Christ.

8. Fresh fire, new anointing, envelope my life totally in the name of Jesus Christ.

9. [Say this severally] I receive fire, I become fire, I release fire in the name of Jesus Christ.

10. Anointing of fire that cannot be insulted, possess me to overflow in the name of Jesus Christ.

11. I am not an onlooker in the arena of power, I am a carrier of God's signs and wonders in the name of Jesus Christ.

12. Fullness of the Holy Spirit, take over me in the name of Jesus Christ.

13. My spirit-man drink divine wine, I want to be intoxicated in the Holy Ghost in the name of Jesus Christ.

14. Power to preach and souls are converted, possess me now by fire in the name of Jesus Christ.

15. Anointing to minister with fire and grace, my life is available, enter in the name of Jesus Christ.

1. [*Say each of 16 – 19 severally with a well-focused mind, with emphasis on* '**enter**']

16. Thou fire of God, my life is available, enter in the name of Jesus Christ.

17. Thou Spirit of God, my life is available, enter in the name of Jesus Christ.

18. Thou power of God, my life is available, enter in the name of Jesus Christ.

19. Thou Spirit of the Prophets, fill me with more of You, in the name of Jesus Christ.

20. Overrunning anointing, soak my spirit in the name of Jesus Christ.

21. Anointing to pull down and to build; anointing to kill and make alive, possess to overflow in the name of Jesus Christ.

22. I receive the heavenly mandate to run through troops and scale over walls in the name of Jesus Christ.

23. Walls of Jericho, gates of brass, bars of iron, hordes of Goliaths, rivers of Jordan and red seas, bow before the name of Jesus Christ in me.

24. Mantle of fire, cloak me now in the name of Jesus Christ.

25. I receive staff of authority and a seal of fire from heaven in the name of Jesus Christ

26. I become an awesome wonder to many. You my life become too hot for the kingdom of darkness in the name of Jesus Christ.

27. In every life aspects and endeavours, I ascend from minimum to maximum in the name of Jesus Christ.

SHOUT 49 HALLELUYAH

DELIVERANCE FROM SPIRITUAL COBWEB

Their webs shall not become garments.... Isa 59:6

You are walking on an open road, and suddenly cobweb lands on your face or arm, then something is wrong. When you are having cobwebs coming upon you in unusual places then, an evil programming has been assigned against you – a programming of rejection and poverty has been set against you.

Or you dream of cobwebs trapping or blocking you.

TEXT:

Isa 59:5 – 6; 64 :16-17; Psalms 25:16; Proverbs 31:9

CONFESSION:

No weapon that is formed against (me) shall prosper; and every tongue that shall rise against (me) in judgment (I) shalt condemn.

This is the heritage of the servants of the LORD, and their righteousness is of me, saith the LORD. Isa 54:17

SING PRAISES

PRAYER POINTS

1. I plead the blood of Jesus Christ, I plead the blood Jesus Christ, I plead the blood Jesus Christ, (say this several times)

2. In your mercy O Lord, attend to my case today in the name of Jesus Christ.

3. Blood of Jesus Christ, usher me out of abandonment, rejection and poverty.

4. Evil covenants with poverty, by the blood of Jesus Christ, break and release.

5. Foundational and generational dedication to spiritual servitude, break by fire and by the blood of Jesus Christ.

6. Evil magnets magnetizing cobwebs of darkness unto me, roast by fire in the name of Jesus Christ.

7. Seed of witchcraft spiders in my body, soul and spirit system, catch fire, roast to ashes in the name of Jesus Christ.

8. Seed of witchcraft spiders on my face, catch fire, roast to ashes in the name of Jesus Christ.

9. [Demonstrate this] Mark of rejection and poverty on my face, on my arms, I rub you off in the name of Jesus Christ.

10. Every cobweb, attacking good things in my life, catch fire in the name of Jesus Christ.

11. Agents of darkness using cobwebs as a weapon against my glory, be arrested and die in the name of Jesus Christ.

12. Satanic network against my life, be consumed by fire in the name of Jesus Christ.

13. Powers, blocking good things from coming to me, die by fire in the name of Jesus Christ.

14. Agents of darkness organizing my downfall, arise, run naked into market places in the name of Jesus Christ.

15. Fabric of rejection and poverty, woven with witchcraft cobwebs, catch fire, burn to ashes in the name of Jesus Christ.

16. Token of rejection and poverty ministering against my glory by witchcraft cobwebs, be aborted by fire in the name of Jesus Christ.

17. Seed of witchcraft spiders in my blood system, catch fire, roast to ashes in the name of Jesus Christ.

18. Chains of spiritual cobwebs limiting my greatness, break fire in the name of Jesus Christ.

19. Where I have been rejected, I am now celebrated, glory of God, advertise me by fire in the name of Jesus Christ.

20. Right arm of the Lord, push forward, pull me upward by fire in the name of Jesus Christ

21. I move from minimum to maximum in the name of Jesus Christ.

22. By fire, by fire, by fire, my name, change from Forsaken, to Beulah in the name of Jesus Christ.

GIVE THANKS FOR PRAYER ANSWERED.

MY HELP AND HELPER LOCATE ME NOW

...that I may shew him kindness for Jonathan's sake? 2 Samuel 9:1

Who was Mephibosheth?

a. He was born into the royal house.

b. By age 5, calamity befell him. 2 Sam 4:4

c. His source of joy, seemed to have ended at childhood

d. He had to escape into exile.

e. He became lame while fleeing. 2Sa 19:26

f. He lived in abject poverty till adulthood

g. Suffering continued even till he had his first child

No help came to him. He resigned to fate to die that way. 2Sam 9:8

Suddenly, a helper woke up one day and remembered him, and washed him and made him to dine with the nobles.

¹ And David said, Is there yet any that is left of the house of Saul, that I may shew him kindness for Jonathan's sake? 2 Sa 9:1,7

Does the description above look like yours? A helper is about to remember you. Help is on your way.

TEXT:

2 Samuel 4:4; 9:1-6, 13

CONFESSION:

Why art thou cast down, O my soul? And why art thou disquieted in me? Hope thou in God: for I shall yet praise him for the help of his countenance. Psalms 42:5

SING PRAISES

PRAYER POINTS

1. Evil tongues in my foundations, disqualifying me as a candidate of divine help, by the authority of the Word of God, I condemn you in the name of Jesus Christ.

2. Voices in my foundations saying 'Not so' to my help and helpers, the voice of the Lord silence you in the name of Jesus Christ.

3. Forces in my foundations, chasing away helpers from me, die by fire in the name of Jesus Christ

4. By the blood of Jesus Christ, ancestral evil marks, chasing away helpers from me, I wipe you off.

5. Veils from the grave, chasing away my helpers from me, catch fire in the name of Jesus Christ.

6. Stench of the grave, chasing away my helpers from me, be washed away by the blood of Jesus Christ.

7. I fumigate my life with the blood of Jesus Christ; stench of rejection in my life, cease!

8. Blood of Jesus Christ, wash off the powder of shame from my face.

9. Ancestral evil guide following me about, stop, die by fire in the name of Jesus Christ.

10. By the blood of Jesus Christ, marks of rejection, disgrace and shame upon my life, I erase you.

11. Programming of rejection, disgrace and shame assigned against my life, be aborted by fire.

12. Every veil covering the mind of my helper from remembering me, catch fire in the name of Jesus Christ.

13. Powers, delaying the moments of my joy, your time is up, die by fire in the name of Jesus Christ.

14. Powers, using my weakness to erode divine help in life, your end is now; die by fire in the name of Jesus Christ.

15. Angel of good tidings, announce me to my helpers, in the name of Jesus Christ.

16. Mercy of God, magnetize divine help and helpers to me in the name of Jesus Christ.

17. Right arm of the Lord, hold my right hand; lead me on unto life fulfilments in the name of Jesus Christ.

18. Oh Lord my Father, my strength cannot do it, take over; I am at my wit's end, take over; in the name of Jesus Christ.

19. Oh Lord my Father, my strength cannot do it, take over; help me in the name of Jesus Christ.

20. Help of God; change my story to glory in the name of Jesus Christ.

21. My moments of rejoicing, I want you now, appear by fire in the name of Jesus Christ.

22. I am a carrier of God's glory, help of God, men and angel; locate me by fire, in the name of Jesus Christ.

APPRECIATE GOD FOR PRAYERS ANSWERED!

I PURSUE, OVERTAKE & RECOVER ALL

David ...went to recover his border at the river Euphrates. 2 Samuel 8:3

David recovered a lost border city from Hadadezer, king of Zobah. You can recover every good, great and lofty things you have lost too.

This prayer is for those who:

> have a slim or no hope or are in hopeless situations

> have lost many opportunities, promotion or admissions into desired positions

> know that they can still have their greatest heart desire fulfilled irrespective of how long it has been delayed.

> are experiencing delayed breakthroughs, pending testimonies and/or hanging blessings

> are sure that they can still recover all they have missed or lost, before the year runs out.

TEXT:

And Jabez was more honourable than his brethren: and his mother called his name Jabez, saying, Because I bare him with sorrow.

And Jabez called on the God of Israel, saying, Oh that thou wouldest bless me indeed, and enlarge my coast, and that thine hand might be with me, and that thou wouldest keep me from evil, that it may not grieve me! And God granted him that which he requested. 1Ch 4:9-10

CONFESSION:

And David enquired at the LORD, saying, Shall I pursue after this troop? shall I overtake them? And he answered him, Pursue: for thou shalt surely overtake them, and without fail recover all.
1Sa 30:8

SING PRAISES

PRAYER POINTS

1. You that stubborn power, saying that my story will not change for the better, your time is up, disappear by fire in the name of Jesus Christ.

2. You the stubborn problems, that started with me from the womb, and want to end my life with me, you are a liar, receive divine solutions in the name of Jesus Christ.

3. You the stubborn challenges, that started with me this year, and want to end my life with me, you are a liar, be overthrown by fire in the name of Jesus Christ.

4. You the stubborn enemies, that started with me this year, and want to end this year with me, you are a liar, depart by fire, die in the name of Jesus Christ.

5. You the stubborn bondage, that started with me this year, and want to end this year with me, you are a liar, break and release me, in the name of Jesus Christ.

6. You that power, postponing my turn-around testimonies till next year, why are you still alive, die.

7. Demonic sacrifices, offered to delay my deliverance, be paralyzed by the blood of Jesus Christ.

8. Captivity of my destiny from the womb, break and release me now.

9. Captivity in my life from the day of my naming ceremony, break and release me now.

10. I receive my deliverance from witchcraft captivity.

11. I receive my deliverance from self-imposed captivity.

12.   My season of tears, expire with this year.

13.   Oh Lord my Father, in Your mercy, wipe away my tears.

14.   Miracles and breakthrough that bring tears of joy, overtake me now.

15.   Grace to recover 40years in just 40 days, overtake my life now by fire.

16.   Grace to recover 40 days in just 40 minutes, overtake my life now by fire.

17.   Before soon, I recover by fire, every good thing stolen from my life.

18.   Anointing of sudden and total recovery, overshadow my life now.

19.   I receive the wisdom to break even at the point of, 'What shall I do?' in the name of Jesus Christ.

20.   I pursue my captors, I overtake, I recover all my goods/health/prosperity in the name of Jesus Christ.

APPRECIATE THE LORD FOR ANSWERED PRAYERS

PRAYERS TO CRUSH AFFLICTIONS AND HARDSHIP

TEXT:

Psalms 34:19; Psalms 132:1 Acts 7:10

CONFESSION:

And the Lord have said, I will bring you up out of the affliction of Egypt unto the land of the Canaanites, and the Hittites, and the Amorites, and the Perizzites, and the Hivites, and the Jebusites, unto a land flowing with milk and honey. Exodus 3:17

SING PRAISES

PRAYER POINTS

1. Sins in my life, opening doors to affliction, be shut by the blood of Jesus Christ.

2. Foundational evil covenants, opening doors of affliction into my life, I break by the blood of Jesus Christ.

3.   Mercy of God, terminate self-destructive habits in my life in the name of Jesus Christ.

4.   On-going programming of self-destruction assigned to cause affliction in my life, be aborted by the blood of Jesus Christ.

5.   My flesh, bones and blood, receive fire, become too for affliction in the name of Jesus Christ.

6. Powers of affliction and oppression, targeted against my life, die in the name of Jesus Christ.

7. Every power that has singled me out, for affliction, die, in the name of Jesus Christ.

8. Serpent of affliction in my body, roast by fire in the name of Jesus

9. Arrows of affliction, backfire, in the name of Jesus Christ.

10.   I reject affliction, in the name of Jesus Christ.

11.   You spirit of infirmity and affliction, lose your hold and depart from my mind in the name of Jesus Christ.

12.   Thunder of God! Break every pot affliction cooking against my life in the name of Jesus Christ.

13.   Every program of affliction for my body and destiny, expire, in the name of Jesus Christ.

14.   My father, cause every instrument of affliction in my body to expire, in the name of Jesus Christ.

15. You messenger of affliction, release your affliction on your sender, in the name of Jesus Christ.

16. O Lord, as you parted the Red Sea, separate affliction from my destiny, in the name of Jesus Christ.

17. Angels of war from the throne of God destroy every power afflicting my life and destiny in the name of Jesus Christ.

18. Arrows of affliction, backfire, in the name of Jesus Christ.

19. Powers of affliction and oppression, targeted against my life, die in the name of Jesus Christ.

20. My father, cause every instrument of affliction in my body to expire, in the name of Jesus Christ.

21. You messenger of affliction, release your affliction on your sender, in the name of Jesus Christ.

22. Every power that has singled me out, for affliction, die, in the name of Jesus Christ.

23. O Lord, as you parted the Red Sea, separate affliction from my destiny, in the name of Jesus Christ.

24. Angels of war from the throne of God destroy every power afflicting my life and destiny in the name of Jesus Christ.

(GIVE THANKS AND WORSHIP THE LORD FOR PRAYERS ANSWERED)

ISH-BOSHETH, LEAVE MY THRONE!

Everyone is created a king, a ruler, a domino. Hence, everyone has a throne. A throne is a seat of influence and affluence; of honour and harvest; and of greatness and goodness, privileges and prosperity.

This throne could be in the domain of academic, vocation, talents, ministry, expertise, government, etc.

For the truth that man is made in God's image and likeness means you are indeed a king or a queen. Genesis 1:26

Irrespective of what low position you are now, that truth remains – you are a king.

So, if you are not reigning in life yet, then it means you are not at your divine location or there's a wrong occupant on your throne. It's time to take back your place of destiny; arise, get angry in your spirit, reclaim your throne.

TEXT:

But Abner the son of Ner, captain of Saul's host, took Ish–bosheth the son of Saul, and brought him over to Mahanaim; And made him king

....over all Israel. 2 Samuel 2:8-9

CONFESSION:

And hath made us kings and priests unto God and his Father; to him be glory and dominion for ever and ever. Amen. Revelation 1:6 KJV

SING PRAISES

PRAYER POINTS

1. Foundational covenants of slavery and servitude, receive the blood of Jesus Christ, break and release me.
2. Foundational signatures of littleness on my ancestry, be erased by the blood of Jesus Christ.
3. Blood of Jesus Christ, silence the voices of idols of my father's house, calling me unto demotion.
4. Curses upon my ancestors, flowing in my life, by the authority of the Word of God, break by fire.
5. I terminate my sojourn in the wilderness of life, in the name of Jesus Christ.
6. Every King Saul, chasing after me, fall down; die by fire.

7. Every Abner that has sworn that I will not occupy my throne, make a mistake, receive double disgrace in the name of Jesus Christ.

8. Stubborn Abners; waiting for my unguarded moments, die by fire in the name of Jesus Christ.

9. Confusion from God, appear between Abners and ISH-BOSHETHs in my life in the name of Jesus Christ

10. Thunder of God, unseat every ISH-BOSHETH, on the thrones of my life in name of Jesus Christ.

11. ISH-BOSHETH on my throne, somersault and die in the name of Jesus Christ.

12. Right arm of the Lord, overthrow evil kingmakers robbing me of my thrones in the name of Jesus Christ.

13. By the authority of heaven, I move from prison to palace in the name of Jesus Christ.

14. By the authority of heaven, I move from wilderness to palace in the name of Jesus Christ.

15. By the authority of heaven, I move from minimum to maximum in the name of Jesus Christ.

16. By the mercies of God, I move from zero to zenith in the name of Jesus Christ.

17. I rule in the midst of my enemies in the name of Jesus Christ.

18. By fire by force, I possess my thrones now in the name of Jesus Christ.

(GIVE THANKS AND WORSHIP THE LORD FOR PRAYERS ANSWERED)

DEFEATING WITCHCRAFT HORNS

What is a horn?

A horn is:

>|a representation of power, dominion, glory, and fierceness.

>| an instrument of attack

>| an agent of suppression

>| a tool of oppression

>| the strength of an enemy

>| a symbol of wickedness

Four horns means:

>| four oppressive and destructive instruments/agents from the four cardinal points of the earth.

>| four domineering principalities from above (in the air), from below (in the ground/water), from the left and from the right.

But heaven has prepared a counter-attack to disgrace witchcraft strengths. Left to the wicked, you don't deserve joy and happiness. He wants your head to remain bowed in defeat. Zechariah 1:21a. But God has your interest at heart; to attack your attackers that your head may be raised up in victory and jubilation.

TEXT:

Zechariah 1 *18 Then lifted I up mine eyes, and saw, and behold four horns. 19 And I said unto the angel that talked with me, What be these? And he answered me, These are the horns which have scattered Judah, Israel, and Jerusalem. 20 And the LORD shewed me four carpenters. 21 Then said I, What come these to do? And he spake, saying, These are the horns which have scattered Judah, so that no man did lift up his head: but these are come to fray them, to cast out the horns of the Gentiles, which lifted up their horn over the land of Judah to scatter it. Zec 1:18 - 21*

CONFESSION:

Behold, they shall surely gather together, but not by (God): whosoever shall gather together against thee shall fall for (my) sake. Isa 54:15

SING PRAISES

PRAYER POINTS

1. Carpenters of heaven, appear, and destroy every horn, making my head to bow in shame, in the name of Jesus Christ.

2. Wicked horns of my father's house; wicked horns of my mother's house, making my head to bow in shame, break by fire, in the name of Jesus Christ.

3. Witchcraft representatives assigned against my life and family, scatter and die in the name of Jesus Christ.

4. Witchcraft glory in my life, die in the name of Jesus Christ.

5. Host of heaven, appear and overthrow every dominion of darkness operating in my life in the name of Jesus Christ.

6. It is written, 'No weapon formed against me shall prosper..', witchcraft instruments formed against me, catch fire in the name of Jesus Christ.

7. Witchcraft cauldrons, cooking my destiny, catch fire, scatter in the name of Jesus Christ.

8. Witchcraft arrows, fired at me, backfire in the name of Jesus

9. Every voice summoning me from witchcraft coven, by the voice of the Lord, be silenced in the name of Jesus Christ.

10. Witchcraft ropes, tying me down to the same spot, catch fire in the name of Jesus Christ.

11. Like the altar of Jeroboam, the son of Nebat, altars of darkness, carrying anything that represent me, break and scatter.

12. Evil hands, pressing me down in my sleep, wither by fire.

13. Agents of witchcraft, hired to pull me down, fall down and die.

14. Agents of the marine power on contract against me, receive a sword of fire, die in the name of Jesus Christ.

15. Evil priest, wicked priestess, offering sacrifices against my destiny, on witchcraft altars, die by fire in the name of Jesus Christ.

16. Lord arise, and crush the strength of witchcraft powers waging wars against my life in the name of Jesus Christ.

17. Back bone of my stubborn enemies, receive hammer of fire, break in the name of Jesus Christ.

18. Instruments of oppression, working against me, I defeat you now.

19. Witchcraft tongues chanting incantations against me, wither, die

20. Logo of witchcraft, sending away my helpers, catch fire

21. Witchcraft stickers, upon my forehead, I peel you off by fire

22. Witchcraft trophies scatter by fire.

23. Witchcraft powers, oppressing me from the north, die by fire.

24. Witchcraft horns, attacking me from the south, die by thunder.

25. Witchcraft powers, spoiling me from the east, die by fire.

26. Witchcraft horns, opposing me from the west, die by thunder.

27. Witchcraft dominion, oppressing me from the air, crash land, die.

28. Witchcraft powers, stealing from me from the moon, the sun and stars, crash land, die.

29. Powers, oppressing me from the grave, die by thunder.

30. Marine witchcraft, oppressing me from the waters, die by fire.

31. Powers, oppressing me from the left, die by thunder.

32. Powers, oppressing me from the right, die by fire.

33. Wickedness programmed against my glory, be aborted by fire.

34. Witchcraft powers, that had disturbed my ancestors, you can no longer not get me, die by fire*Witchcraft powers, that had destroyed, my neighbours, you will not get me, die by fire.

35. Anointing of fire to pursue, to overtake, and recover all, fall upon me now in the name of Jesus Christ.

36. You that witchcraft horn assigned to bow my heads in ...., did by fire in the name of Jesus Christ.

>| defeat

>| failures

>| no testimony

>| near-success

>| inherited bondages

>| frustrated efforts

>| disfavour

>| disregard

>| fruitless labour

>| shame

>| incurable sicknesses

>| marital turmoil

>| barrenness

>| depression

>| dishonour

BREAKING THE SHACKLES OF SPIRITUAL SLAVERY AND SERVITUDE

And the LORD shall make thee the head, and not the tail.

Deuteronomy 28:13a

Felix works under a boss for 5 years. His boss notices that his business begins to flourish as soon as Felix joins the workforce. Felix has the charisma, the intellects and the positive attitude it takes to turn anyone's business around. At the end of the 5 years, Felix decided to be his own boss. He applies all it takes but his own business fails. He returns to the boss. The boss's business gets transformed again still through him. He spends 2 more years there and re-started his own. He still can't make it. One day, Felix cried to bed and dreamed – he saw himself wearimg lofty clothes but there was a big slave collar around his neck.

This is an example of spiritual slavery and servitude. There are these sets of people that they can't just be their own boss. Other sets can never and harvest beyond average life.

And it shall come to pass in that day, that his burden shall be taken away from off thy shoulder,...

Today is the day.

TEXT:

Joshua 9:21-27; Jeremiah. 28:2; Isaiah 65:21-23; Deuteronomy 28:13; Nahum 1:9-13; 2Chronicles10:4; Lam 1:3

CONFESSION:

And it shall come to pass in that day, that his burden shall be taken away from off (my) shoulder, and his yoke from off (my) neck, and the yoke shall be destroyed because of the anointing. Isaiah 10:27

SING PRAISES

PRAYER POINTS *(Please you will need anoint oil during this prayer)*

1. My foundations, the blood of Jesus Christ is speaking to you, respond now.

2. Ancestral evil dedications of my father's house, the Blood of the Lamb is speaking to you, respond now.

3. Inherited sins in my ancestry, the blood of Jesus Christ is purging you now.

4. Curses in my ancestral lines, the authority of the word is against you now, break and release me in the name of Jesus Christ.

5. Ancestral handing-over of my glory, be overturned, be revoked by the blood of Jesus Christ.

6. Sell-outs of descendants by my ancestors, my case is different, I have been redeemed by the blood of Jesus Christ, be reversed now by fire.

7. Inherited ancestral debt, be annulled by the blood of Jesus Christ.

8. Spiritual slave masters, Jesus Christ is my new Master, loose your hold from me, die by fire, in the name of Jesus Christ.

9. Chains of spiritual slavery, fetters of spiritual servitude, break and release me by fire, in the name of Jesus Christ.

10. Placental attachments tying me to the ancestral lines, catch fire, in the name of Jesus Christ.

11. *(Please demonstrate 11 – 12)* Stigma of spiritual slavery and servitude, I peel you off, catch fire, in the name of Jesus Christ.

12. Verdicts of spiritual slavery and servitude, I tear you up in the name of Jesus Christ.

13.   Decrees of spiritual suppression and subjection, catch fire in the name of Jesus Christ.

14.   Pharaoh of my father's house, die, in the name of Jesus Christ.

15.   Marine witchcraft chain, holding me down to the same spot, break and release me now, in the name of Jesus Christ

16.   Evil hands, that always drag me back to square one, like the hand of Jeroboam the son of Nebat, wither by fire in the name of Jesus Christ.

17.   Tokens of transfer of spiritual enslavement into my life, die by fire, in the name of Jesus Christ.

18.   By fire, by fire, by fire, I remove my neck from inherited shackles of spiritual slavery and servitude of my ancestors, in the name of Jesus Christ.

19.   By fire, by fire, by fire, I remove my feet from the fetters of spiritual slavery and servitude of my fathers, in the name of Jesus Christ.

20.   I reject it by fire; I shall no more toil before I eat, in the name of Jesus Christ.

21.   I reject it by fire; I shall no more be a second fiddle in life, in the name of Jesus Christ.

22.　I pronounce my freedom from backwardness and spiritual servitude in the name of Jesus Christ

23.　By the power that delivered Israel out of Egypt, shackles of spiritual slavery, break by fire in the name of Jesus Christ

24.　I shall not be little, I shall not be small, my moment of greatness, appear by fire, in the name of Jesus Christ.

25.　I am not a servant, I am not a slave, I am not in bonds, I am a freeborn in Christ Jesus Christ.

26.　I shall no more labour for another to eat in the name of Jesus Christ.

27.　Right arm of the Lord, lift me up and keep me up in the name of Jesus Christ.

28.　*(Get oil, anoint your hands and decree on the two hands)* You my hands, as you have prospered while I am serving others, you shall prosper while I am serving myself in the name of Jesus Christ.

29.　Thou labour of my hands, begin to experience unimaginable prosperity in the name of Jesus Christ.

30.　I shall no longer labour in vain in the name of Jesus Christ.

GIVE PRAISE TO THE LORD FOR PRAYER ANSWERED.

PRAYER FOR DIVINE ELEVATION

See, I have set thee over all the land of Egypt. Genesis 41:40b

No ordinary hands can elevate anyone to an enviable height ; it's the divine hand of the Lord. Joseph was lifted from prison to prime minister's seat; Mordecai from a gate guard to a royal PA.

That hand behind the rising of the sun is set for you.
It's your turn to be lifted.

Then Pharaoh sent and called Joseph, and they brought him hastily out of the dungeon: and he shaved himself, and changed his raiment, and came in unto Pharaoh. Thou shalt be over my house, and according unto thy word shall all my people be ruled: only in the throne will I be greater than thou.
And Pharaoh said unto Joseph, See, I have set thee over all the land of Egypt. Gen 41:14, 40-41

TEXT:

Genesis 45:8; 1Samuel 2:7; 2Samuel 7:8; 1Kings 14:7; Psalms 75:7; Daniel 2:21

CONFESSION:

But thou, O LORD, art a shield for me; my glory, and the lifter up of mine head. Psalms 3:3

SING PRAISES

PRAYER POINTS

1. Blood of Jesus Christ, ransom me out of the dungeon of life.

2. Blood of Jesus Christ, redeem from bondages that my characters has positioned me in the name of Jesus Christ.

3. *(Demonstrate this)* Arrows of littleness; fired against my head, I shake you out by fire, in the name of Jesus Christ

4. Sword of fire, locate that marine chain holding me down, cut it off and set me free in the name of Jesus Christ.

5. Witchcraft veil covering me from the helper of my destiny, catch fire in the name of Jesus Christ.

6. *(Hold your two hands close to your mouth)* Curses of failure upon my head and upon the works of my hands, shall NO MORE prosper in the name of Jesus Christ.

7. Every agent of shame in my life, die, in the name of Jesus Christ

8. Foundational powers that stunt my promotion, die in the name of Jesus Christ.

9. Territorial powers that delay promotion, die in the name of Jesus Christ.

10. Environmental powers that cripple promotion, die in the name of Jesus Christ.

11. Internal altars that stunt my promotion, die in the name of Jesus Christ.

12. You that power that waits for me at the edges of my breakthrough, your time is up, fall down and die in the name of Jesus Christ.

13. Anointing of the tail upon my life, I cut you off, die by fire in the name of Jesus Christ.

14. Power of divine promotion fall upon me, in the name of Jesus Christ.

15. I mount up with wings as eagle, I soar high in the name of Jesus Christ.

16. I receive divine wind under the wings of my destiny in the name of Jesus Christ.

17. Fire of promotion fall upon me, in the name of Jesus Christ

18. Power to ride above the storms of life, possess me now in the name of Jesus Christ.

19. Helpers of my destiny, remember me by fire in the name of Jesus Christ

20. O Lord that answereth by fire, promote me by your fire, in the name of Jesus Christ.

21. My gifts, my talents, showcase me for divine elevation in the name of Jesus Christ.

22. Thou power of God, that lifted Joseph from prison to palace, lift me up by fire in the name of Jesus Christ.

23. Thou power of God, that lifted David from sheepcote to the throne, my glory is available in the name of Jesus Christ.

24. Thou power of God, that lifted Jeroboam from the backyard to the courtyard, lift me up by fire in the name of Jesus Christ.

25. By the power of the Holy Ghost, I am remembered me for good today, in the name of Jesus Christ.

26. I move forward by fire, in the name of Jesus Christ.

27. I reject the spirit of the tail, in the name of Jesus Christ.

28.   My head, receive favour from God, men and angels, in the name of Jesus Christ.

29.   Anointing for divine wealth fall upon me, in the name of Jesus Christ.

30.   Oh Lord make me a candidate of your divine promotion, in the name of Jesus Christ.

31.   Anywhere I go, I receive favour, in the name of Jesus Christ

32.   I receive my letters of promotion by fire, in the name of Jesus Christ.

33.   You my letters of promotion, you shall not be taken away from me any longer, in the name of Jesus Christ.

34.   My destiny, be promoted by fire in the name of Jesus Christ.

35.   I move from poverty into my divine prosperity, in the name of Jesus Christ

36.   Oh God of Abraham promote me above my adversaries, in the name of Jesus Christ

37.   I refuse to go back to the enemy, in the name of Jesus Christ.

38.   Right arm of the Lord, pull me higher, push me forward and keep me steady in the name of Jesus Christ.

39.   Power of God, move me from zero to zenith; from minimum to maximum; from average to excellence in the name of Jesus Christ.

WORSHIP THE LORD FOR ANSWERED PRAYERS

PRAYER TO DISCOVER HIDDEN SECRETS

Ye ask, and receive not, because ye ask amiss... Jas 4:3a

A problem known is half-solved. Knowing the secrets behind a challenge of life exposes it to a faster solution and a more effective remedy.

...because ye ask amiss. Praying to know hidden secrets helps to pray targeted prayers. It could also be a wise thing to pause that prayer you have been praying for too long and pray this one to know why the answer to your prayer seems delayed.

You may need to ask God what next/else to pray in order to get that testimony you so much desired.

TEXT:

Deuteronomy 29:29; Daniel 2:22, 47; Psalms 25:14

CONFESSION:

Surely the Lord GOD will do nothing, but he revealeth his secret unto his servants the prophets. Amos 3:7

SING PRAISES

PRAYER POINTS

1. Every pollution, every contamination of sin causing spiritual blindness in me, be washed away by the blood of Jesus Christ.

2. By the blood of Jesus Christ, I receive divine pardon for every unrighteousness in me that is pushing the spirit of revelation far from me.

3. *(Raise up your hands to the heavenly) Blood of Jesus Christ, cleanse my hands.*

4. *(Cover your eyes with your hands)* I wash my third eye in the blood of Jesus Christ.

5. Programming of spiritual blindness, functioning against my life, be damaged by fire, in the name of Jesus Christ.

6. Holy Ghost fire, laminate my third eye in the name of Jesus Christ.

7. Scale of spiritual blindness, catch fire in the name of Jesus Christ.

8. Arrow of spiritual blindness, fired into my spiritual eye, jump out with your poison by fire, in the name of Jesus Christ.

9. Deposit of spiritual blindness in me, catch fire, in the name of Jesus Christ.

10. Spiritual blindness in me, die by fire, in the name of Jesus Christ

11. Deposits of spiritual cataracts, catch fire in the name of Jesus Christ.

12. Satanic veil covering my inner-man, catch fire in the name of Jesus Christ.

13. My spiritual antenna, receive fresh oil in the name of Jesus Christ.

14. O Lord, give unto me the spirit of revelation and wisdom in the knowledge of You in the name of Jesus Christ.

15. O Lord, make Your way plain before my face in the name of Jesus Christ.

16. Light of the Lord, reveal the hidden details behind this matter in the name of Jesus Christ.

17. Light of the Lord, expose the concealed details behind this challenge I am passing through, in the name of Jesus Christ.

18. O Lord, bring to light anything planned against me in darkness, in the name of Jesus Christ

19. Hidden covenants in my life, be revealed now, break by the blood of Jesus Christ.

20. Hidden curses in my life, be revealed now, break by the blood of Jesus Christ.

21. Hidden bondages in my life, be revealed now, break by the blood of Jesus Christ.

22. Like unto Daniel O Lord, make me a vessel of divine revelation in the name of Jesus Christ.

23. Fire of the Holy Ghost, incubate my eyes in the name of Jesus Christ.

24. Spiritual road blocks to vision, dreams and trance in my life, be dismantled by the finger of God in the name of Jesus Christ.

25. Every ancestral secret retarding my revelational ability, be exposed in the name of Jesus Christ.

26. Evil secret activity currently affecting my life, be exposed and be disgraced, in the name of Jesus Christ.

27. Every secret I need to know to excel spiritually and financially, be revealed in the name of Jesus Christ.

28. Every secret hidden in the marine kingdom, affecting my elevation, be exposed and be disgraced, in the name of God.

29. Every secret hidden in the satanic archive, crippling my elevation, be exposed and disgraced, in the name of Jesus Christ

30. Every secret I need to know about my environment, be exposed in Jesus Christ' name

31. Every secret I need to know about my father's lineage, exposed, in the name of God.

32. Every secret I need to know about my mother's lineage, be exposed in the name of God

33. Every secret I need to know about my home town, be revealed, in the name of Jesus Christ

34. Every secret I need to know about the work I am doing, be revealed, in the name of Jesus Christ.

35. Oh Lord, make Your way plain before my face on this issue in the name of Jesus Christ.

36. Oh Lord, reveal to me every secret behind this particular issue in the name of Jesus Christ.

37. Holy Spirit, reveal to me the deep and the secret things about….. in Jesus Christ name

38. Anointing of spiritual illumination, revelation and direction, come upon me now, in the name of Jesus Christ.

39. Like unto Elijah, Thou still, small voice of the Lord, speak to me, I am listening in the name of Jesus Christ.

WORSHIP THE LORD FOR ANSWERED PRAYERS

DELIVERANCE FROM HOUSEHOLD WICKEDNESS

Yea, mine own familiar friend, in whom I trusted, which did eat of my bread, hath lifted up his heel against me. Psalms 41:9

Household wickedness? They are found within the family; children of the same mother or/and father, amongst friends, neighbours, spouses, children or parents or even house helps, drivers or gatemen. People who dine and smile with you; people who you feed or feed you; so close to you like the veins in your neck. Yet they could be the clog in the wheel of your progress or the Absalom that sets your farm on fire.

TEXT:

Judges 16:18 Psalms 41:9; 55:12 Micah 7:6 Matthew 10:21 24:10 26:16 Luke 22:22,48 John 13:21, Numbers 12:1-3, Judges 15: 9-12, II Samuel 15:13,

CONFESSION:

Mine enemies speak evil of me, When shall he die, and his name perish? Psa 41:5

SING PRAISES

PRAYER POINTS

1. Mercies of God, journey with me in this prayer, in the name of Jesus Christ.

2. Blood of Jesus Christ, flow against the evil strongman of man of my father's house.

3. Blood of Jesus Christ, flow against the evil strongmen in my vicinity.

4. Monitoring gadgets of the wicked powers of my father's house, roast by fire.

5. I withdraw my secrets in the custody of the wickedness

6. Eliab of my father's house, receive divine padlock

How do you know a Household Wickedness Personality?

i. They give wrong, destiny-destroying advise

ii. They are very envious. Joseph's bros,

iii.   They are covetous. Absalom

iv.   They say discouraging things

v.   They don't see anything good in you

vi.   They are very close to you. Absalom, Miriam and Aaron

vii.   They are merciless. Joseph's bros

viii.   They eat from the same plate with you

ix.   They are betrayers. Delilah, Judas, Ahitophel

x.   They usually team up with outside enemies

xi.   They are despiser of good things

xii.   They are people you least expect. Absalom, Miriam, Aaron

xiii.   They are usually those owing you favour; those you have helped before. Absalom and Ahitophel

What are their Operations/Who are they?

a.   Envious rivalry Gen 37:11

b.   Evil enquirers Gen 37:17a

c.   Conspirators Gen 37:17b

d.   Mockers Gen 37:19

e.   Destiny destroyers Gen 37:20a

f.   Dream killers Gen 37:20b

g.   Destiny traders Gen 37:27. Joseph's bros; Delilah

h. Destiny destroyers

i. Destiny thieves. (they steal thrones. E.g. Absalom) II Samuel 15:13

j. Fear famers. Eliab to David. 1 Sam 17:28-29

k. Opportunity blockers. Eliab

l. Unfriendly friends. Delilah, Ahitophel

m. Witchcraft barbers who shave off glory

n. Evil reporters

PRAYER POINTS

1. Every mother of witchcraft in my family, what are you waiting for? Die in Jesus Christ name.

2. Every spirit of "I have to do it", in my family die, in Jesus Christ name.

3. Any power eating my food and drinking my water but planning for my destruction, loose your power in Jesus Christ name.

4. Every padlock of witchcraft in my family, burn up, in Jesus Christ name.

5. Every witchcraft hand that carried me as a baby, I judge you by fire, in Jesus Christ name.

6. You mountain of darkness that is hindering my progress, die, in Jesus Christ name.

7. Every plantation of witchcraft on my father's side, what are you waiting for? Die, in Jesus Christ name.

8. Every seed of witchcraft on my mother's side, what are you waiting for? Die, in Jesus Christ name.

9. Every witchcraft embargo on my finances, die, in the name of Jesus Christ.

MY VISA, APPEAR BY FIRE!

¹Now it came to pass on the third day, that Esther put on her royal apparel, and stood in the inner court of the king's house, over against the king's house: and the king sat upon his royal throne in the royal house, over against the gate of the house. ² And it was so, when the king saw Esther the queen standing in the court, that she obtained favour in his sight: and the king held out to Esther the golden sceptre that was in his hand. So Esther drew near, and touched the top of the sceptre. ³ Then said the king unto her, What wilt thou, queen Esther? and what is thy request? it shall be even given thee to the half of the kingdom. Esther 5:1 - 3

CONFESSION:

⁷ Lift up your heads, O ye gates; and be ye lift up, ye everlasting doors; and the King of glory shall come in. ⁸ Who is this King of glory? The LORD strong and mighty, the LORD mighty in battle. ⁹ Lift up your heads, O ye gates; even lift them up, ye everlasting doors; and the

King of glory shall come in. [10] Who is this King of glory? The LORD of hosts, he is the King of glory. Psalms 24:7 - 10

SING PRAISES

PRAYER POINTS

1. Covenants with disappointment, break by the blood of Jesus Christ in the name of Jesus Christ

2. Every witchcraft curse working against my traveling overseas, break in the name of Jesus Christ name

3. Holy Spirit, disgrace every household enemies waging war against my traveling abroad in Jesus Christ name

4. Evil voices saying NO to the procurement of my visa, by the voice of the Lord, be silenced now in the name of Jesus Christ

5. Marks of rejection upon my life, be erased by the blood of Jesus Christ

6. Every evil embargo placed on my traveling, be lifted by fire in the name of Jesus Christ

7. Every satanic checkpoint in the second heaven against my breakthrough be dismantled by fire in the name of Jesus Christ

8. Every power sitting on my traveling somersault and die in the name of Jesus Christ

9. I withdraw my passport from every evil alter in the name of Jesus Christ

10. Ever satanic bodyguard monitoring my traveling for evil die in the name of Jesus Christ

11. I reject every satanic conspiracy against my visa in the name of Jesus Christ

12. Every stronghold at the edge of my breakthrough, be dismantled in Jesus Christ name

13. Every failure mechanism designed against my destiny, die by fire in the name of Jesus Christ

14. Every satanic padlock fashioned against my visa scatter by fire in Jesus Christ name

15. Windows of heaven open for my visa in the name of Jesus Christ

16. I cancel with the blood of Jesus Christ, every dream of rejection in the name of Jesus Christ

17. I cancel with the blood of Jesus Christ, every dream of hatred in the name of Jesus Christ

18. Holy ghost inject my blood with the virus of favour in the name of Jesus Christ

19. Anointing for favour, fall on me in the name of Jesus Christ

20. Every failure at the edge of my Visa breakthrough, die in the name of Jesus Christ

21. Every curse of rejection, my life is not your landing space

22. Every Pharaoh from the waters, sitting on my traveling somersault and die

23. You my passport, being to magnetise your Visa in the name of Jesus Christ

24. Every mark of rejection on my passport be erased by the blood of Jesus Christ

25. O Lord, grant me favour before the Consular Officers in the name of Jesus Christ

26. I pursue, I overtake, and I recover everything stolen from my life in the dream

27. Holy ghost fire, promote me in the name of Jesus Christ

28. My visa manifest by fire in the name of Jesus Christ

29. I am favoured by God, I am favoured by heaven, I am favoured by men by fire in the name of Jesus Christ

SAY, THANK YOU JESUS 21 TIMES

ABOUT THE AUTHOR

Adedamola Adedokun is a Pastor in one of the branches of Mountain of Fire and Miracles Ministries in Nigeria. He is a man of grace, worship and prayer. He is a trained deliverance minister and an avid Bible scholar.

ABOUT THE BOOK

Prayer Conquest series is a collation of prayer points that the author has been posting since many years on his blog, DELIVERANCE BY FIRE. As at the moment of publishing this book, the blog has more than 275,000 page views.

This book is meant to have these prayer points handy anywhere you go, even when you are not connected to the internet.

Many visitors who visited the blog are sharing testimonies of how these prayers have blessed their lives. We solemnly trust the Lord that it blesses yours too.

We await your testimonies. Happy praying!

Printed in Great Britain
by Amazon